SONO

WITH

VISITS FROM THE SEVENTH

SARAH ARVIO

SONO

WITH **VISITS FROM THE SEVENTH**

INCLUDES CD OF *SONO*
READ BY SARAH ARVIO

BLOODAXE BOOKS

Copyright © Sarah Arvio 2002, 2006, 2009

ISBN: 978 1 85224 844 4

First published 2009 by
Bloodaxe Books Ltd,
Highgreen,
Tarset,
Northumberland NE48 1RP.

www.bloodaxebooks.com
For further information about Bloodaxe titles
please visit our website or write to
the above address for a catalogue.

Bloodaxe Books Ltd acknowledges
the financial assistance of
Arts Council England, North East.

Cover design: Neil Astley & Pamela Robertson-Pearce.

Printed in Great Britain by
Bell & Bain Limited, Glasgow, Scotland.

ACKNOWLEDGEMENTS

This edition includes the whole of *Sono* (2006) and selections from *Visits from the Seventh* (2002), both first published in the US by Alfred A. Knopf, New York, and reprinted here by kind permission of the publisher and author. Sarah Arvio reads *Sono* on the accompanying audio CD, which is first published with this edition. The recording includes all the poems in *Sono* except for two ('Roma' and 'Goose') which could not be included for reasons of space. The CD was produced by Rigel García de la Cabada, and edited and mastered by Evan Younger, Lewis Center for the Arts, Princeton University.

Sarah Arvio wishes to thank the editors of the following journals, anthologies and online reviews where the poems in *Sono* first appeared or were later reprinted: *American Academy in Rome Society of Fellows News* ('Head'), *The Antioch Review* ('Cross', 'Lessons'), *Archipelago* ('Traveling', 'Shadows', 'Thesaurus', 'Grace', 'Grief', 'Hope', 'Veronica', 'Trauma', 'Sistine', 'Song'), *The Cortland Review* ('Chagrin', 'Obelisk'), *Harvard Divinity Bulletin* ('Renaissance'), *The Kenyon Review* ('Park of the Doria Pamphilj', 'Starlings'); *Literary Imagination* ('Cant', 'Petrarch'), *The New York Times* ('Matter'), *Nuovi Argomenti* ('Green Market', as 'Mercato delle Verdure', translated into Italian by Damiano Abeni), *Poetry Daily* ('Acrolith', 'Amourette' and 'Pantheon'), *Poetry Kanto* ('Grace', 'Lessons', 'Hope' and 'Armor'), *Pequod* ('Bomb', 'Veronica'), *Southwest Review* ('Grotesque'), *The Threepenny Review* ('Acrolith'), *Verse Daily* ('Grotesque', 'Starlings'), *The Washington Post 'Poets' Choice'* ('Amourette') and *Women's Work* ('Starlings'). She thanks the American Academy of Arts and Letters and the American Academy in Rome for the John Guare Rome Prize Fellowship, during which most of these poems were written.

She thanks the editors of the following journals and anthologies in which the poems in *Visits from the Seventh* first appeared or were later reprinted: *The Best American Erotic Poems: From 1800 to the Present* ('Mirrors'), *The Best American Poetry 1998* ('Floating', 'How We Yearn', 'Denmark', 'Death', 'Temptation' and 'Rêves d'or'), *Columbia* ('Love'), *The KGB Bar Book of Poems* ('Mirrors'), *Literary Imagination* ('Fame', 'Reverence'), *The Paris Review* ('Floating', 'How We Yearn', 'Denmark', 'Death', 'Temptation' and 'Rêves d'or', winners of the Bernard F. Conners Prize for the long poem, as well as 'Hats', 'A Leaf', 'Murder', and 'Ellipses'), *Raritan* ('Memory', 'Côte d'Azur'), *Southwest Review* ('Clouds'), and *The Washington Post 'Poets' Choice'* ('Love'). She thanks the MacDowell Colony and the Corporation of Yaddo for fellowships held during the writing of *Visits from the Seventh*.

She also thanks the editor of *Poeti e Poesie*, where nine poems from *Visits from the Seventh* and *Sono* were reprinted, alongside Italian translations by Antonella Anedda.

CONTENTS

SONO

cantos

Traveling

I'd been ostracised, so I hid my head.
And what was the view from under the sand;
it was a view of the Interior,

it was an Interior Ostracism.
It might have been a desert or a beach.
What if I said the world was my ostrich,

when I'd hoped to say it was my oyster;
what special muscle did I like to eat?
And what oyster was my sovereign world?

Spin the globe to Africa or Austin...
Was I a gawker, was I a creeper,
was I a stiltman, was I a sleeper?

Was this my world; it might be the oyster's.
Having it all in the palm of the hand
or in the palm at the end of the mind.

This was traveling and seeing the world;
there were verbs: to oyster and to ostrich.
Sand of the desert and sand of the sea,

each had its beauty, each had its place.
And yes, sand in the meat of the oyster,
and yes, sand in the meat of my own mind.

I gathered around it and made my pearl,
as pure as something made of grit can be.
This was Australia or Austerlitz;

here was an extravagant *ostrakon*
with the shell as the sky and the blue-and-
pink stain as sunset and the rim, what else,

as heaven. And this: lie in the desert
a little longer. Or sleep on the beach.
Then leave your shells behind you in the sand.

Matter

I was what mattered in the end. Or if
I didn't matter then nothing mattered,
and if I mattered, well then all things did.

O miracles and molecules, dust, rust.
It was always a matter of matter.
It might be meat or else it might be love

(if I was meat, if I was fit to eat).
What had never been matter would never
matter: you might say this was a moot point.

Clay and dust, ash and mud and mist and rust,
blood-orange sunsets and turning maples,
apples and cherries, sticks and trash and dust,

rumpled papers blowing across a street
(*dead letters sent to him that lives away*).
There was life, there was loss, there was no such

thing as loss – there was nothing that wasn't
both life and loss. No, it had to be said,
in questions of matter, nothing was lost.

It might be a matter of carnal love.
This was textual and material,
and for once the facts-of-the-matter were

both heartfelt and matter-of-fact. (Oh,
matter of course was always the mother.)
These were the facts of life, this was my life,

and there I was, right at the heart of it,
my own heart – at the heart-of-the-matter.
And did I matter now or in the end?

O mother, maintainer and measurer,
mud and fruit of the heart, meat of the heart,
the question might be asked, what was the end.

Fiesta

This much I found to say: I was afraid
facing the future to face the future.
What fool did I hope was my fortune, what

fortune or fact did I hope was my fool;
what fundament was wrong with my fortune.
Fashion me, I said, a fate I can fête,

fashion me a fate I don't have to hate,
diverting and no, never desperate,
and yes, find me a fund of fun, fun, fun

– a funicular not a funeral –
for going up, up, up and not down, down.
O phantom heart, phantasmagoria,

I had forgotten one word: forever.
A day, hello a flag, again a flag
wearing the colors of the inner heart.

Love, a forest of flags waving for me,
bending and blowing in the wind like flames,
a fiesta of flames burning for me,

turning and tossing in the wind like flags.
It was all such a factual feeling
and there was my fear in point of this fact.

It was a desire that had to be had,
actualised in a factual act.
The question arose, or the question fell:

was it no longer desire when it was had.
Oh fond, fond – fountain of my flames and flags,
a moment later it might have been had.

Green Market

The grocer was looking strangely at me.
Your aura, he said, pointing to my head:
you've got all the colors of the garden.

Radish and carrot, tulip and turnip,
some horticultural dynamism
in the arc of my ulterior glow.

A sovereign rarity, my soul rays,
spread out on my head like a color chart.
I matched the rainbow, the summer sunset,

the green flash, the lightning, the green-cheese moon.
– So was there a green market in heaven?
No, not at all, that was a blue market,

because blue was saved for the sea and sky,
blue was saved for the bottom of the soul:
in heaven they only ate blueberries.

What did I know, what could I ever know;
could I see the blue dark inside myself,
the dark occasion or my own third eye.

I could see the eye but never myself,
even with the help of a mirror or muse.
What use was vision if I couldn't see.

A celery stick might be nice with salt,
some celerity, some hilarity,
a sprig of parsley or a spinach leaf,

a green flag waving in the cosmic wind.
He'd learned to live, he said, without desire
(not an achievement for most of us). As

he gazed at my aura, I watched his eyes.
I saw desire; he was kidding himself
and maybe therefore he was kidding me.

Shadows

I saw some shadows moving on the wall
and heard a shuffle, as of wings or thoughts.
I rolled back the sheets and looked at the day,

a raw, blown day, white papers in the street.
Sheets were flapping in the sky of my mind,
I smelled the wet sheets, I tasted a day

in sheets hanging in the damp of a day.
White pages flapping: my life had been so new
when I didn't yet know how old it was.

I couldn't see the vistas on those sheets,
the dreamscapes sleeping deeply in those sheets;
I hadn't yet seen my shadow vita

or learned which host would trick me or treat me,
which of my hosts would give me something sweet,
some good counsel and a soft place to sleep,

or what was the name of my ghostwriter.
Who ghosted my life, whose dream would I ghost,
who wrote my name and date across these sheets,

and which sheets would be the wings of my thoughts,
and which would hold the words of my angels.
A host, and did I know I'd have a host;

no, a line of sheets is never a bed,
a gaggle of hosts is never a love,
a host is never as good as a home,

a ghost as good as a dog or a god.
But I had my heart, always had my heart
for god and a home as much as it hurt.

Roma

Though the home, we say, is where the heart is,
wonder if the heart is where the home is.
Had I found a heart for my home and did

I live there and love there: this was the point
that all roads should lead to if I traveled.
This was the question that was romanesque,

or else something random or romantic;
this was the ancient question of amor,
was it Rome and home and could I live there.

Here was a hurrah and a holiday,
all the domes planting a star in the sky,
all the domes pointing upward and somewhere,

all the crypts sinking downward and nowhere;
but did they point and did they also pierce,
did they crack the shadow or the sunshine.

Chiaroscuro of the coffered heart,
or the yes and no of the offered heart.
Did I fit with it, did it fit with me,

was I its shadow or its positive,
was I its pentacle or palindrome.
The point was to see there was no point

or was the arrow pointing to the heart,
a road sign, a feather or a weapon.
There was a dome and a home, there was Rome,

and for every recto there was verso.
One lives to live and that's the best we know,
and then dies to die and then it's over.

Thesaurus

Given a way would I be this; given
this thing would I be this. I never knew
how persons could be things, and yet we were

in the vast cosmic Thing; we were little
things. There were greater animations than
ourselves, and to them we were things. This was

a thought in the forest of – thesaurus
of – my nomenclature. How often had
I thought, am I alive or am I dead,

never knowing what either Thingness was.
These were the woods we were talking about,
these were the words we were talking about,

where the forest was always in the trees,
where what I saw was always what I was;
my words, some leaves, all bristling with my life,

animate and *aimée*, all that was all.
There was an aura, call it a halo,
call it the glow of the moment of grace;

there was something oracular and old,
there was the show and glow, there was hello,
there was yes, no, there was congenial

and genial and joy. There was genius,
a genie in the bottle, breath in the lungs,
there was more than just being as I was:

wind in the woods, a forest in my mind,
the mind of my life found in the forest,
the Thing being named my thing, as it was.

Grace

Somewhere over in the platonic place
where I was enshrined in my high ideal,
was there a pure depiction of myself

written in water or else on the wall,
a plural entity named for my grief
or named for my excursions into joy,

some Cerberus or trio of Graces
gracing my life with a howl or a dance,
some triangle of me, myself and I,

an altar to an alternating self
alone, alert beside the aqueduct –
an allusion to the trope of Sarah,

aleatory emblem of my all
as wind spit rain through the ancient arches
and cloud faces gleamed in the dark-lit sky.

There was now and then, there was yes and no,
there was gracious and there was also grave,
but was there a place for my gravity,

where the wall and the wind were in myself,
or a continuum of my own self,
graceful Cerberus, cerberean Grace

gravitating toward the heart of a want,
a place to create what I longed to be
– or the planet versus Platonism –

all the faces of my envisaged self,
engraved with weather, my wish and my will,
gravid with 'luminous intensity'.

Grief

So, was there something grand in all this grief,
some grand canyon or great cathedral vault,
some grand arcades and avenues and walls,

ringing with echoes, hello and goodbye,
the hoofs of centaurs and centurions.
The little griefs were the gauge of our lives,

the glass of water waiting to be drunk,
the stick of wood wanting to be knocked,
a sliver of glass, a splinter of wood.

Luck, luck, it was always the same lament,
what I never got and what I gave,
what I never gave and what I got.

I had always wanted to grace myself
with a garden growing before my eyes,
a riot of grandeur and abandon.

If you want a big thing, oh take a grave,
if you want a grand thing, oh take a life,
try out a garden, try out a grave.

Ha-ha ha-ha, there was the big guffaw,
a hundred halos and a hundred hells,
a great load of guff and a lot of gall;

there was Dada, there was Dionysus,
daimon, duende, a darling or a dog,
god and love, or a horse or a hope;

there we were, gaga at all forms of god,
there was godliness and there was a dog,
yipping at my heels, yippee oh yippee.

Scirocco

Was I allowed to be alive, was I
allocated to life, was I alive,
was I a specimen of the species:

these were the questions I asked myself
while the scirocco was thrashing the sky,
raining red leaves and raining orange sand.

Was I dust, dirt and sand, dare I be dust,
there in Africa where they swept me up
off the orange drifts of shoulders and hips,

off the drifting dunes where bodies were heaped,
lying in sleep, shifting in sleep and dream,
where I dreamed I was a specimen

born to be special and specialised,
as all specimens of the species were,
while dusk flames and dawn flames climbed on the dunes

in an ambience of rage artistry
or an arrangement of orange and red
artfully arising; was I dead or

alive; was this my allowance of life,
my own modicum of *become become*,
my scirocco my barocco of rage.

There were candle flames, there were cigarettes,
amber whiskeys, amphoras of *I am*,
there were amulets of *I am I am*;

there were orange flames, red leaves, orange sand,
moons, mornings; there were moments still to burn
back in Africa where they swept me up.

Flames

What might have ruined me, that I became,
rising, as they say, from ruins or flames
– gaudy flames of *I am I am I am* –

a fire of me refusing what I was
and watching that one self burn and become.
These were such flagrant and flamboyant words

– overblown, overburned words – but were true:
blue and green, flaring to yellow and red,
red flags, yellow rags, oh fluttering wings,

flaming some red-hot downright refusal.
With my hand reaching up against the sun
and taking the shape of a leaf or flame,

I blocked the light or I watched as it burned
around my splayed fingers or through the leaf.
All my words scorched in the heat of a fight,

leaf, leaf and flame, watching them rise and go,
goodbye, goodbye, preparing for hello;
all the hells lived, these could be my hellos,

all the hellions of the self I was.
Oh my dantesque demons, now say goodbye,
all the grandiose, grandiloquent griefs.

How sad to say goodbye to what I was,
also of course to what I might have been –
gorgeous glories going up and away.

Stage

Did I have a genie or a daimon
to usher me onstage or sweep me off,
my own dear harbinger or usherette?

Curtains! came a cry, and the curtains shook.
Here was a masquerade *en abîme*,
a hidden histrion hamming my lines

deep in the jewel box of my drama,
angeloform, deiform or magic.
O angels ruffling your wings in the wings,

which of you is my own special angel?
Why not have the courage of Coleridge
to say it was a dream or a vision;

it might be a wish or else an anguish,
it might be an image or a language.
Was it anecdotage or sabotage,

was it chanson or could it be chantage.
Historical or else hysterical
or else ancestral or angelical.

Was this the character I often shunned,
so sultry and desperate and ravaged;
was this the character I often wished,

oh my little magus oh my cabbage;
was this verbiage or genius or madness.
No rehearsals: you get only this chance,

one call for this life, one cue for this love
(know how to bow in and how to bow out),
you did it or you didn't, that's the play.

Grotesque

(for Susanna Moore)

Freud had offered common unhappiness
but I know I wanted uncommon joy;
godly or ghostly, what help could be had,

was there a helping hand, was there a god.
There was grace, the only cure for grief,
the submission to the heart of your god,

to the heart or hand of a friend or god,
some giving in, the gift of giving in,
as common as the grackles and starlings.

As though hello could be a harbinger,
as though happiness could be happenstance,
saying holiday, saying holy day,

something lifting in the house of the heart.
And did I have a star, did I have a grail,
did I have the necessary grotto,

the grassy knoll, the grove, the granite bench,
for making my anguish into a wish,
for turning grief into grotesqueries –

meaning shape-shifters, meaning shadow art,
or hilarity in the house of god,
of god or the kings, that was my own house

if you believe the 'thou' of the Quakers.
And all things that might shake or might quake,
as things did when they came into their own,

quiver and quake, and open in the air,
or burst a bud, or break an egg or seal,
or shake a frisky tail, or wave a crown.

Lessons

Hadn't I already learned my lessons,
by now didn't I know what I should know
for living a life? If only I had

learned what I should have or maybe unlearned
what I should never have known, if only
I had forgotten, lapsus, lull – limbo

between knowing and never having known,
though never knowing meant being new.
Laconic scholia of learned life,

undulating from newness to knownness.
There was no new lily, little person,
no new lily in the emperor's pond,

though the lilies kept budding and bursting.
There was no new life in the library,
except for my own, lurking there alone,

late or too late, as all the lessons were;
because the life-hour never came again,
'never to this life would it come again'.

There was the island of the emperor
that lay inside the lily-padded pond,
there were the rest of us lilliputians

puttering near the limen of our god,
articulating and annotating.
Island, island, O pupil of the pond,

don't tell me the emperor wasn't god:
god might be a cloud or an emperor
and even god couldn't begin again.

Hope

I said this: would you give me back my hope
if I suffered hard enough, if I tried.
That hip-swinging hallelujah of hope,

that hip-hip-hooray we were talking about,
raying outward from the hip or the heart,
holistic, holy – those were all high things –

hyper-radical and hyper-real,
that gospel of helix and radiance.
Hail me, hail me, here I am alive,

falling from the lips of the lioness,
lambent and loved, gamboling like a lamb,
having gambled all my griefs and lost them.

Game of the gods, gamine of the cards,
inhaler of hashish and helium.
Here was the hub of the halo again,

the hub or nub of the halo or heart,
and the trope of turning to say hello;
we always said it 'helio-hello'.

Hello to the little girl and lambkin,
garrulous, hilarious, all grown up,
nibbling on nothing and feeling okay,

and sweetly holding hands with the harpist,
turning toward the sun, turning toward the sound
– my warp of the world, my harp of the heart –

sounding like myself, as I always sound,
snappy and stylish and too sonorous,
a little savage and a little sweet.

Cross

I was saying I never had a care,
meaning maybe that I was free of care,
or else meaning that no one cared for me,

but I loved all of you the same as me.
As the Christians said, love unto others,
love others if they believe as you do –

love them, my love, if they'll carry your cross,
crisscrossing the field of your destiny.
Neither Giambologna nor Morandi

is still making art in Bologna, though
they worshipped there at the altar of art
and then died in the service of their lord,

god of stillness and volatility.
By that was meant the art of moving air,
of sitting or lying down or flying,

a set of bottles or a pair of legs
standing or else hanging or lifting off,
or a field full of grasses and crosses.

O caryatid O my katydid,
did you once carry my world or my cross?
Look, my legs swing one across the other,

as a kind of cross, a cross I could bear,
walking across town or swinging my foot,
or a cross, as I said, that would bear me –

my own long legs that were holding me up.
There were days, I said, when I didn't care,
either standing so still or leaping up.

Renaissance

I meant I was and I had always been
the thing I was, though I wanted to be
another version of what being was.

Ha! That would be a busman's holiday,
or getting a buzz on, we used to say,
or borrowing from the bees or the birds

(*and to do that to birds was why she came*),
doing or being, been there and done that.
But it didn't mean lunching on thrushes

and swallowing songs from a songbird's throat,
or else driving in the back of the bus
or else being driven from up ahead.

Drive yourself to distraction was a thought
related to both being and doing.
These old thoughts were coming to me in droves –

not to make too much of a metaphor.
But there was no new news under the sun,
no new news and even fewer songs;

maybe newness was what I didn't want,
maybe only a dose of otherness,
which didn't mean death or eternity.

O wing O wing, and all the flourishes
arranged so neatly on my shoulder blades,
exotic and ornate on my plain back,

and as rideable as a Persian rug...
It was laughable but reassuring,
this tender fillip of the Renaissance,

Filippo Lippi painting in the wings,
a flitter or a flutter now and then,
and the announcement of a coming thing.

Bomb

Was I playing it in the hope of joy,
play it as it lays, as someone said,
playing it down or else playing it up,

or was there some other raison d'être,
some other raisin drying in the sun,
or some other reason under the sun.

Please excuse my French, was there a reason
for being and doing anything else,
dreaming or dying for anything else.

'Be content with lack of misery'
was a kind of motto for some of us,
a kind of bonbon or a platitude,

or a kind of candy for a sucker
when what you need is a drink of sense,
the mot juste and a drink of joy or juice.

Drink up, drink up, or else drink it down,
have you ever pondered the difference?
Not a bon mot or else a play on words

but a choice between rising and falling.
Or lay it aside, play it as you can,
when what you need is some balm for the heart,

or else a pillow for your pretty head,
or a pill, or a grape plucked from the vine.
Maybe a surge, a surfeit or an urge

or something urgent in the argument,
as though reasoning could be part of it:
some say a surge of joy might be killing.

Acrolith

I had been hoping for a change of scene,
surfing the centuries for something new,
like a new head for an ancient body

or a new body for an ancient head
dredged from the sea or a sarcophagus,
or like a new tooth for a tired smile,

iconic or else maybe ironic,
in gold or silver, in plaster or stone,
some metallurgy or mimicry,

a simulacrum or a simile,
like deadheading a favorite rose
or else starting again from the sourcebook.

Sorcerer! Will you give me back my source,
give me a head or let me get ahead;
maybe only a shift of mood or heart,

a goblet of wine and a gulp of air,
a milestone on the road to Nirvana.
Wasn't Nirvana the goal of the nerves

or a hill town on the outskirts of Rome,
a headstone on the highway to heaven?
All this searching for a surge of surprise,

when all I found was as old as the hills.
Surgeon! A splurge, a surfeit or an urge
to bring me to my senses or stun them,

some salvage from the ruin of myself,
some saving grace, a means of saving face –
the face-lift of a Roman fantasy.

Head

No, I was thinking I would lose my head
when there was the emperor's man, and thwack –
it wasn't my hat that was missing.

I was a sister or I was a saint,
maybe a gilded statue of Venus,
sporting a halo or wearing a hat,

blood on my bosom or no blood at all,
gilding a lily or a gala gown;
I was the garderobe or the avant-garde

with the guards at my back in the palace.
What was a bust without a head on it,
what was a dress without a girl in it,

a dress or a bag, a drape or a rag.
Dear Lesbia and poor fat Drusilla,
an emporium of décolletages

or a model of empiricism.
No, 'please save me' wasn't a noble thought,
but save my face, at least that act of grace!

All this was heady, which didn't mean smart;
it was the foam or the fizz, or the fat,
the cut of the gown, the slash of the neck.

Oh god, how I wanted to dance and dance,
dress in a lily, shake myself silly.
The thought wriggled up, but my head was gone.

It could be me or my image in stone.
It might be a headstone or a hanger,
a headache maybe, or a hangover.

Colosseum

That was the blood again, the selfsame spot
that had to go – which didn't mean the rose,
though blood and a rose could share a color.

It rose to my face, as a blush would do,
for showing you that I was what I was.
I was the empress or else the goddess

or the servant of my sensual thoughts,
and I threw all my meat to the lions
to be eaten alive or lionised.

A colossal mess I made of my life,
in the flesh and also in the round;
this was the essence of colosseum,

the museum of my colossal shame,
where I mused on the blood sport of it all,
where I longed for the lust of the lions.

Here was my game, the name of my sin,
for I never threw men to the lions
or rose from my lair or ate men like air,

or pearls to the pigs, though I tossed a rose
to the crowds and begged them to spare my life,
dominion and dungeon of the senses,

and all the beauty and the blasphemy.
Petals, petals, scattering from the stands
where only vestals were allowed to sit,

having tended the flame for all of us.
Here, I knew, was the empire of my soul
showing on my face as I turned to you.

Veronica (Vera Icon)

I was walking on Via Veneto.
Va-va-voom! he said, and I laughed out loud:
it was all in the verve of the gesture.

I was a green-eyed blonde, I was a girl.
Vainglory! Will you give me some of it,
garrulous, god-struck, full of vinegar.

This might have been a visionary stance,
a revision of Isis and Venus,
reversion to a vision of grandeur,

or desire in a raw and vital state,
another variant of verismo
and as vivid as a green valentine.

Viva! Some green blood running in my veins,
te quiero verde (I want you green),
which didn't mean I want you virtuous

if virtue meant veiling your truer thoughts.
Or maybe virtue was Veronica,
an adventure in the vernacular,

passing her handkerchief, tossing her cape.
One was a swinger, one was a saint,
one was devoid of all vanity and

one was standing in the path of the bull:
it was all in the quest for victory.
There was vanitas, there was veritas,

I hoped I had both guts and godliness.
Some of us had more and some had less –
this was the true truth we were green about.

Sine Qua Non

I was wandering in a quandary
and never without a qualm or a pang,
and thinking of taking a quantum leap

out of my quondam life and into yours.
Not, I didn't say, my goddamn life, I
said my own life I didn't care to live.

Not to be quarrelsome, quote me on this;
who were you anyway, who have you been,
my quotient or quorum of joy or jazz.

I said your life, which was a better one,
or would have been, dear love, with me in it.
My sine qua non, where did you wander?

I took a gander, and that was my life
(oh where was Juno when I needed her),
a quiet gamble on my golden eggs,

on the qui vive for a kiss or a hand,
asking the question, the querulous one,
like who lives and who loves and how do they.

Quo vadis, as history often asked;
the answer, always, was I'm going back,
looking for a goose, a lamb or a duck,

a croon or a cluck, a quid for my quo.
This was quackery, I mean a bad fix,
dumb luck, my destiny or a dumb fuck,

many beautiful fucks, quote me on this,
meaning fucking you again and again
and being fucked by you, which was the same.

Trauma

I was trammeled, I thought, by tragedy,
oh what, something long ago, some travail
of my soul or my body, or of both.

The 'little tragedies of daily life'
tremoring through me – tremor wasn't a verb,
tra-la-la wasn't either, or trial,

though they trailed through my life, didn't they,
a tracery of tears, a track of woes.
Woes, woes, ten little fingers and toes,

decades of them, this deed, that distortion,
a tort against the treasured harmony.
A twist or a twirl, a tic, a tic-tac-toe,

thrumming on the synapses, drumming out
a threnody of threats and tears, a thought-
torture, love, love, a tiny tortured heart.

My heart, my own little tap-tapping heart,
my tapped-out heart, their testament to me,
a test of wills, or a test of my will,

my willingness, my wish to weather on.
Oh waves, waves, all the ripples and rhythms,
the rituals of walking and reaching,

the verbiage, the verb-thoughts, try this, try that;
the rites of therapy and talking trash,
the tapestry of tears, the truth-trapeze.

But did I want the truth? Try me, I said.
This is, this was, this should never have been;
reason, thought-treason and some truisms.

John

Oh give me joy, give me a job in life,
not jobbing or jokes or hobnobbery,
love as a job, not a hand job; a life,

said Freud, is a job and a love. Oh John,
join me forever in my jamboree.
This, after all, was my jubilee year.

Or was I jinxed, was I jinxed or jerked
or deviled by some inner jinx or jive;
some deviled eggs and a slice of *jambon*.

I thought my eggs were maybe too deviled.
Was he hobbled by the gist or the junk,
a job-lot attitude toward choosing joy,

was any girl as good as another?
A Janus look, I mean facing two ways,
toward love and away judiciously;

or Juan, a kind of dungeon of love
(oh be jolly oh be jaunty and brave).
Now I was thinking I would egg him on,

but I got egg on my face, as always.
The mumbo-jumbo, the jumble, the mum,
mumbling love, may I give you my jewel,

the Juliet from the Ethiope's ear,
my lips, my laughter, my adjurations.
Leave your door ajar, and I'll come in.

Let us adjourn, I mean call it a day,
or a night, do let us call it a night
while the jasmine still blooms in the garden.

Graffito

after 'Amat qui scribet'
  (for Kristina Milnor)

Would you engrave my body with your hands?
I would be grateful – I would be so glad –
if you would etch me for eternity

with all the vicissitudes of your hand
and some vision and some vulgarity.
Let me lie here now in a dusty box

with all your vim and love inscribed in me,
may I be scratched here, and then gather dust.
Oh let me first be loved, and then be lost.

Who reads is fucked, and I read you right out,
let me read you again all over me.
Who criticises, sucks – or so he said –

we know it was a man who wrote these things
with a stylus or maybe with a stick
on a gray wall – on yellow or blue –

or on Neapolitan red or pink –
with a pocketknife or maybe a pick.
Engrave me also with some gravitas

and some caritas and some veritas.
He who writes, loves – caring, grave and true.
Write me with grit and grace, may I say this,

here where the graph may be the holy grail.
Let's grapple with the beasts – that is, *the bears* –
let them tear us – write it! – *from limb to limb.*

36

Amourette

It lasted many moons – in fact decades –
but, you know, never morphed into marriage.
Slow amour, as slow as a snail,

and as armored as an armadillo.
Was imperfect love a peccadillo,
or wasn't it love, this purgatory;

in the end I think I was mortified.
Speaking of *petite mort*, there was also
petty murder. O ambrosia. I was

amortised, you know, or slowly murdered
while waiting for a metamorphosis.
It was disarming that it was over.

There was harm in him, and a dose of smarm –
that I wasn't dead was the miracle.
I wasn't quite dead, but almost, you know,

arm over arm with my malefactor.
And, you know, alarmingly amorous.
In marital, martial and lunar law

the dead girl can't marry her mortician.
No one was left but the Necromancer,
not the Romancer and not Amore,

something like heavens to murgatory,
and all the morphology of remorse.
To think purgatory led to heaven!

An armchair, *mon cher*, not a chariot,
all that old passion put out to pasture
for grazing, you know, on "past" memories.

Fix

Fixable, it never was. I knew that.
Or too late to fix by the time I knew.
Fox hunting, a red fox lost in a fog.

Field – fog – fuck. Oh love, was this fantasy.
Va fan culo. As always, go get fucked,
when, after all, that was what I wanted.

My love, a love of fun, a fantasy,
my own fox tail switching in the fog. A
fierce desire, a red tail lost in the snow,

red, white, and the gray branches overhead.
Filigree, fond searches – some fact-finding.
It might be better not to have a fact,

better a totem or a factotum,
an emblem of the general desire,
a handyman or a fox of all trades,

to fix me this or maybe fetch me that –
maybe some thunder or a fundament.
Though there was rarely thunder in a fog.

Fogged in, foxed. No, I wasn't faking it.
Fox, fox – they used to call me that – fine girl –
fetching – they once said that too. Oh love, love,

fetch me a forkful or a fingerful,
a figment or a fig, fetch me a fix.
Oh damn foxation and thunderation,

expectations and fixabilities.
But then, after all, this was my whole life:
I had a thunderous desire to be.

Obelisk

I do believe I was never loved. I
was never loved. An outright blasphemy,
saying so point-blank and out of the blue,

an observation I wanted to make,
maybe too obvious to bother with,
or a bagatelle – too banal to tell –

one little beauty who was never loved,
as blue as a bag lady and as black
as the occupant of an oubliette,

maybe an octopus but not of bliss.
I was blame-emblazoned, my obloquy,
and as bellicose as an obelisk,

as black as a sack, as sick as a sock,
this blah-blah-blah, the soul of lullaby.
Obliteration, that old oration,

blanketing my blue soul, my blue, my soul.
I gave you this oblation to belief,
or maybe obviating disbelief,

and not a ball – no, never a ballet.
I gave you my bold hope, my openness,
as oblong as a long embattled day,

I got a bellyful, I got a beaut –
not to be oblique: a banana fish.
You know you blasted me a round of blanks.

But after all, what was believable
if not my own blue soul on a black day,
when all the beloved were so blasé.

Chagrin

It wasn't the life I would have wanted,
had I known what sort of life I did want,
as if anyone ever knew; though I

did know. Everyone had her shadow life,
her should-have life, the life she should have had,
all those thoughts sharp-sharking into her soul,

all those doodles on the skin of the day.
The shame, that this had been and this had not,
could-should, kowtowing to the life of should,

the shock, let's say, of seeing it had passed,
the chagrin, let's say, the savage chagrin
that this was what it was, et cetera,

who did I think I was, et cetera,
the queen of Sheba in her shantytown,
or Shirley in her temple (*such a doll*),

or Scheherazade waking to the day –
not Sylvia, not the sylvan huntress.
The whole shebang was a shambles, hello,

shanghaiing my wishes, shout it out, shout,
those stories of what was and never was,
love, voyage, give me succor – sugar – suck –

hushing the heart and shushing the senses.
Hello, day, shake the sheets out, wake the day.
Cheers! (As I said this I was choking up.)

The challenge of cheerfulness – hello, charm –
charade and charm, chameleon, cameo.
I saw the dawn and fell into a hush.

Sybil

I thought I would, yes – or no, I wouldn't –
surrender to these thoughts, this thought-surfeit.
In the service of survival, I thought

I would live on the surface of my life,
or surf, let's say, on the waves of my life
– so fun – and so forth – alas – selah –

Some sophisticated sortilege for
shooing off the insinuating snakes.
O Sybil, will you save me from my self-

surrender, and my sacrifice to – what – ?
Sulfuric vapors at the mouth of hell.
In what sense did Sappho survive her life?

She was slain by her life, as we all are.
Let me safari to the farthest shore,
let me hunt sapphires and never suffer.

This weird, solemn world, my word and my way,
this savage world and my self-slavery.
A zephyr blowing – a slow fire – the fat

soprano singing shrilly in her cave –
zaftig – oh so fat – inwardly a sylph.
Sympathetic symphony of sad facts.

Enough of this slavish salivation!
Let me pour out a lavish libation,
let me simmer saffron in a slow stew,

some salve or salvation for Sylvia.
O Sybil, show me something I don't know,
surprise me with some savvy funny news!

Cant

I said I could never live here, and I
never could, but I did for two decades –
I had fallen into a decadence.

No, not a cadence, though that too could fall,
darkly – ever so darkly – through a glass,
or a mirror or a dirty window

barred like a skeleton, barred like a cage.
Not as though I didn't care – I did care.
I had been carping on the debacle

for most of ten years in the candlelight,
the decorum of the core of the deed,
decked in desire, here in my dark cave –

decorated with me, or with my core,
the dark card of the dark lass and lady,
dandling on her lap my own life – my life –

while I combed through the old crowns and papers.
It was tiny but cavernous, it was
cadaverous, it was my catacomb.

But could I be decanted from this jar?
Cant! Cant! The cant of I can't – no, I can't –
comb out my hair, climb out of my lair and

dance with the wind in the dandelions.
If the door was ajar, would I go out,
a cat darting her head around the door

(carpe diem, carry away the day).
A canticle of anticipation,
some dandelion wine and a draft of air.

Petrarch

Oh me, who was my enemy: only
me. I was enacting an anarchy
of me when what I know I needed was

an artfulness. The conundrum of my
innerness – or the eardrum of my me,
always listening to my inner hum.

Oh heart, a sense of humor please, a sense
of inner human humor, a rumor
or a ruffling of happiness. Drum roll:

the conundrum of my cunt (*so sorry*),
the drumming in that inner room – alarm!
Disarm the scaffolding – O arcanum –

and unfold the arch, my architecture,
all the textures of my folded temple
and all the ruffles of an ecstasy.

A penny arcade and some archery,
and a parakeet and a parapet,
the sky above in every color and

a carpet changing colors with the sky.
Pet, pet – could I whisper it to myself
while Petrarch was whispering to Laura

out there on the autoroute to Arqua?
Could I save myself with an arch remark,
could I call myself out on the carpet?

Sistine

I was moving from crisis to crisis
all through my life, with a few calm days
between them like a caress or a charm

descending unexpected from above.
Up there, god's hand was pointing toward Adam
when it could be turning toward the Sybil.

Who cared for love when there was wisdom?
All that stuff in my satchel full of scrolls –
a chrysanthemum or a chrysalid,

for crying out loud, wasn't that enough.
Crystallising the future as an eye,
lifting up the future as an eyelid,

always gazing with a critical eye.
But how sad not to have loved the Sun God
when he might have given me all I wished.

What was so bad about a night of sex?
Here I was, hanging shriveled in my cage,
saying I want to die – want to be dead.

Oh cry sister – or else just suck it up –
or spend some time with Savonarola.
Maybe it was just those sulfuric fumes

rising from deep in the Stygian swamp
that caused my sad moment of misjudgment.
When all the while a mere stanza or two

might have saved the day, saying I love you
– eternities ago – or maybe not.
Or was there still time for some kiss-and-tell,

or some scissoring schism of the heart.
Come down to Cumae and open my cage.
Sad! I had forever but not a kiss.

Song

I said I couldn't love and it was true,
not a ploy, or coy. I couldn't love or
sing. Not canti or canzoni or chants

or airs – not – I could do sex but not
without love, and I couldn't love so I
couldn't do sex. Oy, oy, as the Jews say,

no love and no song, that means no joy.
Happiness, you once said, is not a goal,
it's a happenstance. It happens to some

and not to others. It may have happened
sometime to Mina Loy, or to Myrna,
or to Terry Malloy, but not to me.

Life without love is life without love, as
dry as a stick; it's sick, though saying so,
my love, is cloying. It's not worth a stick.

La, la, I sometimes almost broke into
song – a broken song, could you call it that?
We were drinking rob roys! Those were the nights.

I had inner singing and inner love
but not for me, not for you, I had love
for a boy I once knew but not for you,

never a loyal and unalloyed joy.
This was my stance, and maybe my stanza,
and this was the substance of my romance.

I never could love, now I was oily,
ogling their pants, their hearts, and their hairlines.
Oh how annoying, a blonde with no beau,

an old girl with no toy and no ally.
Oh boy, boy, I know I broke your heart
with my broken song. I know I was wrong.

Tara

Scarlett, I always knew we were the same,
but who was I talking to, saying this,
to you, Scarlett, to you, but who are you,

turning to Tara as I turn to me,
looking I guess for some help from the land,
when the land of course was only my heart,

or hoping for a turn for the better
while turning the soil, when for all that time
the dirt of my soul was talking back. Crows!

They seemed to be everywhere, crowding in,
stalking the furrows whenever they could,
going up one row and then down the next.

We were sumptuous girls, belles of the ball,
a harem of men hanging on our skirts
as long as they did, and then they were gone

harum-scarum, having crowed to our hearts.
So if I were you I would sell myself
for a house or a heart – be a harlot!

With a lot of hair and those freckled hands?
Starlet, will you lend me a barn or a stair,
but I am you and I don't guess I can.

I might buy up a nightclub in Harlem
and listen alone to some scatty jazz.
Scarred, would you say, or scared? Oh my land,

I'm not sure I can scare up a sale;
did I once tell you this was harrowing?
There were horrors and then there were horrors

and no, this was not really one of them.
I guess I'll take a furlough from this field
and hang up my old dress on your scarecrow.

Tempest

I had a flash of insight: there weren't
all that many years left in my life, it
was now or never or never or now.

Full fathom five my father lay but I –
I was standing in the eye of the storm
and it was seeing me or me it, or

neither of us was seeing the other.
I'm telling you I needed a sea change
or to see some change, if change could be seen.

I was just a tempest in a teapot
but I liked my tea, I liked me; my life
was the life I wanted to like. It was

tempting to feel there was something out there,
a flash of lightning or a jag of truth.
Here was the pathetic fallacy and

here was Ariel in his gust of air,
spinning and turning and dancing in air.
But I was slim-bodied and full-breasted,

and tired of my island, my eye, my land,
and no, I didn't need a fallacy!
And no more pathos! (It was *pathetic*.)

I needed a phallus – but not on me –
and not in the elements or heavens.
A flash in the flesh and not in the pan!

And now Miranda stepped into the sun
and gazing away at her strange new world,
poured out some tea for you, her prince, for you.

Goose

Was it over now, I wanted to know,
was it gone, you know, was the game up,
or was I still game, speaking of pheasants,

was I a partridge or a parakeet.
Was I simmering or no, was I stewed
in my own juices, or was my goose cooked.

This was the *wild goose on the barren branch.*
Got your goose, I think someone once said,
and yes, mine was gotten. But not the one

that laid the golden egg. No, not that egg.
Not as good as gold or as gold as straw,
and not the needle in the golden stack.

Not passing through the eye, or through the gates
of horn or gold, or through the pearly ones.
Was I saying I wanted to be dead

or just saying I wanted some heaven –
the rich man in the eye of the needle
or else a dance on the head of a pin

or just a rich man, thank you, that heaven,
or else five golden rings instead of one.
Looking for a partridge in a pear tree

or only a pear, or maybe a pearl
in my oyster or an oyster in my soup.
Looking for a pear in a partridge tree

or some golden eggs left on the beanstalk.
Was I as good as gold, or was I old,
could I lay some gold myself, could I live?

Starlings

All winter I watched the swarms of starlings
swooping in the northern sky like cast nets
or some foreign alphabets flying loose

and returning and rushing out again.
I wanted to live the life I desired,
as we all did, I think, our one desire,

wanting to do what we wanted to do,
sweeping and then spreading and turning back.
A flood of arrows, dare-arrows, daring to hope,

never horizontals or verticals,
not a straight arrow or as the crow flew,
though life, I think, looked daggers at me,

daring me write this letter now to you,
scratching the sky with a row of my words
(*those letters sent to him that lives away*).

Look me daggers, love, stare me in the eye,
dare me to love you and I'll dare you back.
Darling, I will say, my starling, my crow –

no, not a thrush as the century turned,
though I felt a rush looking at the sky
and all the devastations of desire,

as staggering as ever – startling, true,
or dulled, I think, by the drift of the years
or the drag of the years dragging me back

through the smudges of my alphabets,
cirrus clouds like rags cleaning up the sky
and the vast waste of my wasted desire.

Armor

I am nothing if I'm not a lover,
a loved love; we are nothing if not that;
I wasn't but *I am* if you'll let me

be your amphora and your amulet.
For there were days to live and days to love,
meaning there was still a lot of life left

for us, for me if you were there in it,
and maybe you would be and maybe not.
This was the question for me, of our amour,

our armor, the mind and body that we
wore, or were, the armor of our arms and
more, the morphology of our amour.

There was only this life, this love of ours,
together as we were and as we are,
armed and firing in the line of fire.

We were amateurs in the art of love,
you *ami ami* and me, you and me.
Here was shape-shifting in the truest form,

meaning more than form and more than us,
rubbing the stones in our pockets for luck.
Those lucky in love were lucky in life.

A great view of the city lay below
this statue to our metamorphosis,
a monument, my love, to love not war –

ambling arm in arm, drinking up the night.
Think if they made statues to love heroes
returning from the Campus Martius.

Park of the Doria Pamphilj

I know I was startled to feel like this,
staring straight into the eye of the storm,
the stone pines turning toward me and away –

stands of them standing, and then bending back,
and showing the filigree of their crowns,
the lace of their brains against the gray sky,

brandishing themselves like many giant wands,
or pinwheels or kaleidoscopes, gray-black,
green-black, showing the inside of their minds,

and not colliding though it seemed they could,
and ruffling the sky with their big green hair.
I was there, I'm telling you, I was there,

and I saw it like a cocktail party:
we were all holding up our martinis
in long-stemmed glasses, looking at our minds,

as wet and dreamy as a stormy sky,
pining for a departure or a part,
a promenade through the ancient city.

I was a madwoman wearing a green hat,
I was a maenad or a martinet,
or a mannequin waiting to be dressed,

and leaning toward my friend the skeleton,
a scope or a decision, or a hope,
pinning me to a purpose or a part,

eliding me with something in this life,
as lean as a stick, reaching toward the sky,
some skeleton or rorschach of a thought,

a potato print or a pantomime:
and being one wanderer, long I stood,
going somewhere while rooted to the ground.

Pantheon

If I had known the pleasure principle,
how different all those years would have been,
all those years I spent plaintive and pleading,

but that was plain pain, that was the pure stuff;
could I sing it as a psalm or a hymn,
a sigh to god or to some other one

to look this way, not that way, and soothe me.
Forsooth and so forth, it did not occur.
I was forsaken, and not for my sake –

for whose sake I'll never know, believe me.
Force of habit, or force of not having,
or perforce it had to be, and it was.

Or peremptory, on the part of who?
Meaning who was it who picked out my part
instead of giving it to someone else,

or phase, passage, it could never be known.
Though pass me a pill, or give me your hand,
hand me a pillow or else a haven,

or read my palm and tell me what you see:
I see a palm at the end of my mind,
swaying like an arm, waving like a hand,

the print of a palm or else a blueprint,
a pantheon or a panopticon,
or the prison or prism of myself,

meaning the one view or all of the views,
or else the one god or all of the gods,
and none of them explained what had happened.

from

VISITS FROM THE SEVENTH

from **FIRST ROUND**

I Floating

I said some nonsense or other to them
and they mocked back, 'but we're your one design',
or 'you're our one design' – which was it?

The pen slipped and capered on the page,
escorted by ripplings in the atmosphere
like breeze with nothing to blow against.

'We wear no form or figure of our own
– a wisp, a thread, a twig, a shred of smoke –
to tell us from the motions of the air.

We'd love to live in even a bubble,
to wrap around its glossy diaphanous,
reaching and rounding, as slinkily real

as a morning stretch or a dance in a field.
But we know only this air, and memory,
once, or several times, removed and turned,

the pang of a once-had, a maybe-again,
that shifting half-light, our home and habitat,
those hours, soft-toned, windless, that favor passage,

the usual relay of twilights. And,
how often a century? The sun eclipsed,
that "created" half-light, not dusk or dawn:

us glowing through, our light, our element,
in which we show best, glow best, what we are.
Yesterday some snowflakes slipped through us,

refreshing kisses passing through our heat.
Ah, we wanted to say. If we could have,
we'd have laughed right out from sheer surprise.'

And what else? 'We've got you to stand for us.'
And I have you, I said, to float for me.

I had been missing them very badly,
that day and that day and the next – and yet
the solace they offered was imperfect,

airborne and volatile. I invoked them,
yes, often, in lieu of human contact.
Not that they weren't human, just abstracted

from humanness on the physical plane.
But why had they deserted me? I knew
the answer: for spurning them out of hand.

But where, in that case, did they swirl off to?
Did they rise higher, higher, and vanish
into some upper ether or did they

betrayingly visit someone else who
might at that moment seem more receptive?
Calling them back after a desertion

was never simple: I had to turn my mood
soft, bright, calm and dreamily attentive;
then, after a time, they would slip back in,

one by one, refiguring their spirals
in those inevitable rows of seven.
Would they, I once found the courage to ask,

weave together and net the air for me,
linking and looping their remembered limbs,
to break softly my falling if I fell?

Cradle me, oh cradle me, I whispered.
That was not a service they could do, though.
Life is so complicated for us here,

so troublesome, really, that I wondered
how they found theirs. Did they love it up there
cutting their spirals into cold fronts and

turning somersaults with the storms? Did they
nestle cozy into their troughs of air,
basking in the serene and glossy heights,

the breathtaking vistas of blue-gray seas,
the pink-tinted cloudscapes, the high music –
Or did they, as we do, long for blankets

and warm bodies? So I broached that question
when they came soft-shoeing back in this time.
'No memory, no thought,' one lipped to me,

'can stand in for the loss of a life of touch.'
Amen, I said, and that's the life I want.
So I brushed the air to be rid of them.

III Denmark

'But how could you tell him? Never ever
have we allowed – have we intimated –
you should share our visits with anyone.'
That's I think the gist of what one said.

'All territories have, never forget,
their own imperatives and covenants,
and the tacit ones. Under the so-called
presumption rule – that's Denmark – we presume

that the broader and deeper sovereignty,
crossing all lines, subsuming all bodies,
aquatic or abstract, will override
interior but lesser requisites.'

I wanted to argue that telling him
was not so different from telling myself.
'Oh appeal, appeal, if you must,' one said.
'We don't mind a hum, a word, a whisper

now and then, alluding to some other…
But outright revelation will only
imperil all that we've done, we and you,
to come to this arrangement – all the hours

at work before dawn in the north country,
the briny, eye-blue Baltic blustering
hard by, the sun rising to never more
than low in the sky, a cold yellow blur

gleaming dull in the iced *fourchettes* of trees.'
So, was that all? Was that the sum of it?
Must I then keep mum or suggestive or
throw over all that they had been to me?

'Stay, stay,' I happened to hear one murmur.
A song sprang to mind: '*Oh, Copenhagen,
wonderful…salty old Queen of the sea…*'
(Or some such.) They beamed, for they liked that thought.

IV A Spring

'Go on,' they say and say. But I don't know
how they mean. It seems a matter of joy:
'Go on into it.' All right, *pester me*,

I whisper back. I find it best to be
prodded into pleasing sensations. (Those
who've gotten the other kind of scolding

know how hateful it can be.) I've listened,
and tried and tried, but as always, *'the will
is not the way'*. (As one so sweetly quipped,

'try forcing a spring to flow.') I guess I
know that now and the knowing is a clue.
'It's just the first in a compendium

of clues no one holds the index to.' 'Yes.'
'A flurry of pure air, then some bubbles,
then a rivulet; the less you tend it,

the more it will rise, redouble and rise,
now a smooth-sliding, cool-flowing river
and sometimes gushing up almost wildly.'

'The will is not the way.' This was their mot,
as usual not all that practical.
But above all else, I should 'reverence

what flows from elsewhere,' and 'how like water,
springing cool among grass blades, parting them,
rising to the rim of the embankment

and finding the first down-flowing passage.'
'The green grass may be just a metaphor,
or also' (laughing now) 'a memory.

No, the landscape doesn't determine us:
joy will also flow from mud or rubble.'
They gurgled and whispered, 'yes, darling, yes.'

v Death

Well, the night is blooming. Death may not be
(as the atheists would have it) nothing
at all, but rather (think many of us
who've abandoned god for a sense of god)

a moment to move through, on the other
side of which to find, no one knows, but more
than worms and darkness. For some, a power
almost to speak – although *speak* may not be

the term in the absence of lips, tongue, teeth.
To say. By some means they implant their thoughts
into a person's mind. Mine, for instance.
And thus they go on growing and thriving.

At times they only seem to want to chat
or to make florid gestures, curves and sweeps
and curlicues – *esquisses!* Coy promises
– teases of a vision not to be had;

at others they seem to bud or burst forth
with words pushing to be said, and they nudge
and tickle me to say them for them. They're
working on the matter of openness –

not though, for its own sake, as a value,
but so that I'll be more fertile for them.
Not altogether a noble purpose –
but that depends on the nobility

of the thought they're striving to cultivate.
Doesn't the wish to have one's thought thought of
seem vain, decorative? The lingering
effect of having lived well, maybe, and

not being able to leave it at that.
Always one stroke more to add: another
asterisk, addendum or afterword,
sprig after sprig, petal after petal.

And if their thoughts are fine ones (most seem so
these nights) I don't mind helping them out by
letting them do their thinking in my thoughts.
Petals of promise; calyxes of joy.

I like to fancy them as my teachers;
if they use me well, I may even learn
to use myself. And just now the room fills
with a fragrance of flowers. Or of love –

no, that isn't so. And yet, imagine
a garden, not wild but cultivated,
and richly fragrant. Yes, some spring flowers
turned in a breeze: that fresh, that rapturous.

VIII Temptation

I do know the temptation to beg them
to read me the future or to read me
the present so I can parse the future;

and though they may seem to *clairvoient* my mind,
should I trust them to see someone else's?
If they said, 'you are the life of his heart,'

if they hummed, 'he is yours, now and ever,'
or, 'after this hour, he will come to you,'
what if they visioned there not the true thought

but the self-deceit or the subterfuge
and then sang back those thoughts to me? And I
lived my life led by those misreadings?

And what if I said, as I know I did,
where is he now? And they said back 'China'?
What China then? 'A China of the mind,

mandarin and yes, multifarious,
where a hex means merely a hexagram,
where a wild goose perching on a bare branch

means barren love.' Well, was that our China?
Love that I desire return to me
and the change read, 'noblehearted return,'

and return means merely 'turning again';
'return from a short distance,' read the change.
How far had we gone, how far would we come?

Was that then what our China would be?
'The number of sticks is six, the number
for sex, and thus the number of changing.'

'Yes, well, sex *is* a danger to the soul:
it wounds the soul and therefore changes it.
The chaste are always wrong. For sex is change

and change is the essence of everything...'
You see? Such mediumistic moments
were fraught with bad turns, missteps and false hopes.

'The surest bet is to take no counsel
but to love notions in the mere abstract;
to hear *us* as you would hear anyone,

intrigued by the form of the idea
and maybe the manner of the telling
but never taking it as gospel truth.'

'And let's not start now with this silliness
of what-does-it-matter-since-fate-prevails:
for you *do* stand there in the yellow wood

and must choose between two diverging paths,
or many paths diverging from a point,
starting now and moving into ever.'

'Most of us never begin to assess
the infinite ways we never followed,
various in essence and variform,

a vast web of eventualities
traced negative on the verso of life:
verging, converging and parting again,

or radiating from a single verb,
never ever to return or to meet.'
Was it the yellow of the green spring growth,

was it the yellow of the changing leaves,
of summer sun flaming in foliage
and burning the wishbones of the branches?

Was it the rubbed round of the winter sun
lacquering a glare on the frozen snow,
or was it the yellow Indian silk

I wore the last time you made love to me?
The yellow of piss, the refracted rays
in the nubs of the white angora's eyes,

or the yellow of fear – were those woods fear?
Which yellow was it? It was 'all of these'.
It was the 'yellow of your yellow hair'.

But this eludes the question of counsel.
This seems to evade the valence of choice.

XII Clouds

Today they just stopped voicing, all at once,
and then struck up again in a new way,
reminiscent of a distant moment

they wish to remind me they coaxed me through.
Did I mind the switch? Yes, I minded it.
The new tone was so sentimental. Thus:

'Haven't you called us to you, after all?'
'Haven't you needed us in the half-light
of morning, in the gray breach of the day?'

'Haven't you cried to us to come and care?'
'Haven't we sat with you for hour on hour?'
'Didn't we say all the while, *love oh love?*'

'Didn't we loop our names always with love?'
'Oh, yes, we admit it's a bit soapy.
And yet, we will vouch for the truth of it.

Years we waited not far from you, floating;
hoping, hoping for the courage of flowers.
And here they rise in their white-and-green vase,

a cluster of white carnations, long-stemmed:
on each green pole the white flap of a flag,
on each green stick the white puff of a cloud,

each a dream, each a sail on a green string,
a thought as light as a *souffle* of wind,
each an antidote, a contradiction,

of all those many sadder days and ways.
An antidote in the shape of a laugh,
in the form of a word of a white rag...'

Then this: 'We showed you how to turn and curl,
we visioned you how to see in sevens,
we shaped you in the seven shapes of us.'

(I longed to protest that I shaped myself.)
'Not a problem for both are just as true...'
'Are we proud of our design? Yes, oh yes.'

XIII Fame

'We know about your revelation now
and do we mind? It was a precaution
for your sake, not for ours. And after all,

what can we lose out here singing alone?
(Together, rather, but far from censure.)
We're beyond that now – beyond all caring

about convention, if not about fame.'
'Speak for yourself, darling,' another said.
'I craved fame all my life, and don't I still?

But it's best to let the living alone
to enact their own choices, bad or good.'
And, 'oh, yes, the ways I've found to urge them

to remember me leave an aftertaste...'
'Whitman did it, although he must have felt
he was priming his readers to accept

the outré and risqué...' 'And well he should.'
'Yes, but that was before he passed across!'
Oh, and 'after a certain day and hour

all that belongs to......' (here a pause
for one seemed to prefer not to say 'god').
'Please don't forget there's no straight view from here.

We can't simply glance over and size up
the state of our reputations, can we?
Try looking into the slick on the slope

of an airplane's wing when it turns a curve;
try reading your status in the rearview
of a passing car: at the most a glimpse.

Try a pool or try a lake, take a sea.
Take a mirror or take a mind...' (Take me.)
But how rare is such an access? 'Very.'

'And even so, what do we see? At best
only what passes through its medium.'
Through my medium, they mean: what I see.

xv Love

It was not to them I wanted to speak
but they were the only ones who listened.
Do you think I don't know the truth, I said.

Do you think I don't know the half, I said.
I've had half a life to regret all those
regrettable acts of lovelessness. And

did I think he would follow me through them
whispering encouragement, or hissing
not that! not that! I might have hoped it, yes.

But no one could and no one did. I came
alone; I had myself; a bare self is
bare of persons, for they make us ourselves,

they dress us in ourselves. Hope of a self,
to dress in the person of another.
And someplace, in some other, chosen life,

all rival Pamelas shall be unborn,
all plain, brown-haired girls fingering their pearls
with a factual air of what-makes-sense.

'What a waste of words!' But I saw his eyes,
I saw their wander and their wishfulness.
She thinks she got him but she never did.

She thinks she holds him but she never will.
I have him in his sleeping wish and kiss;
she has his truce and loss, his settlement.

In a whisper, one of them said to me:
'Why have you never said to us, *why me?*
Do you take for granted our choosing you?

Do you think that we're your voices and, oh,
of course we choose you, having no other?
Do you still wonder if you made us up?'

I barely recall the beginning now:
one day the pen marked a curl, and the word
read 'love' (often a word worth turning to).

Love, who? The name came, and then 'Here for you.'
The words spooled out. *Oh, is someone?* I said,
life having handed me an unfair share

of such someones. 'Yes.' How they liked the word,
I noted that. 'Yes, yes.' And then followed
the moments of years of half-light visits:

a name, a note, a notion, nothing more,
and the words: 'love, love, love, love, love, love, love,'
in their reassuring crowds of seven.

I knew they came because I needed them.
I weighed their coming by my need of them.
And yet, their criteria were other:

'*We want nerves strained to the edge of a rip,
nerves studied & soothed & almost salvaged,
each in the hold of its own sensation.*'

It sang like a psalm. A pause, and then this:
'We never like to expose this standard
because of all those who might feel prompted

to emulate a pain they never knew,
who might simulate your special status –
not a purpose that sources love or art.'

XVII Reverence

The next night, one put it differently:
'We want reverence and irreverence
in a combination that pleases us:
knowing when to adore, when to subvert...'

'Oh, even rhythm likes that principle.'
And doesn't love? I said. 'Yes, love does too.
It's the little subversions, the teases,
a nip on the neck, a breath by the ear,

that excite us into deeper rhythms...'
('Do we stretch a point?') *That* was what there was:
'What pulsed and then what pushed against the pulse,
running under the surface of the day,

a violence but a sweet violence,
the tactile balance of a savage thing,
in the balance of love.' *That* balanced it.
('So much wilder when contained in the skin

of a person than riding loose out here.')
And now the pen dipped softly: 'Bless your night.
It is not like that of us at all we
who view the burning of imploded stars

who follow the turning of the planets
as though slow around us our blood still flowed.
Bless the blood and bless the man in your arms,
bless the capillaries and bless the cells

for that high heat, that material touch.'
And this: 'Never reach for sensation or
try for ecstasies. In sex as in art,
success, my dear...' The pen stumbled and stopped.

I find a pen in my handbag or I
cadge one from a waiter in some café
(I walk that way almost every day now);

leaning up against the marble siding,
I place its tip on a scrap of paper,
a theater ticket, a credit slip,

even a café napkin, and let go.
They always reveal much muscular joy
at being permitted to have a say,

and the pen loops out, 'yes, yes,' or, rarely,
a vehement 'no.' I gather they *view*
through the verso of any reflection,

through the silver medium of mirrors,
through the backs of eyes: picture that café
through the sight of one who walks – not easy!

The mirrored sides of skyscrapers *do* help,
despite eternal problems of dazzle:
seen from this side, a grid of silver panes

phasing from pale to deep as day passes;
visioned from that side, oh very much like
a lighted stage in a dark theater

and on its boards a look at real New York.
I know they also crave intimate views,
so I pause for a glimpse in my compact.

I always feel an access of rapture
to be heeding them out there on the street,
as *their* voice – as the voice of one of them –

removes from the noise of my other thoughts,
a cool transparency, so clean and clear,
a lot like the clearness of clear water,

as of flows, as of a sense of flowing.
At times I almost cry from my strange luck
(these *are* the sort of tears they handle best);

note that unhappiness doesn't please them
any more than it does anyone else,
for they can pass their thoughts most easily

through a light happiness, a levity,
empty and sweet and pleased to be alive,
a walk a day along Park Avenue.

XIX Mirrors

A while later that night they flurried in;
some were humming and laughing nervously.
'Have you assessed the deep indecency

most of you tend to feel at having sex
before the spread of a mirror? As though
another couple were in the room and

couldn't help peering at your pleasure or
peeking in your eyes? Who wouldn't flush red
at the sight of two bodies moving in

rhythm both with each other and with you?'
'But under that blush lies a deeper one –
the subliminal, sublunary sense

of being observed from another sphere.'
'Thus the preference for modest mirrors,
hung well above the scene and frame of love,

which enhance the room's depth, yes, but offer
at best an oblique view to a watcher
at a higher vantage.' 'And note that those

who get a thrill from curling and rolling
before mirrors are voyeurs or else want
to be seen by voyeurs, which amounts to

the same thing: a racy view of others'
raptures or lascivious exposure
of one's own.' Now the rills of laughter lulled:

'Despite our pleasure at reacquaintance
with breasts, balls, and lips, it is considered
in cosmic bad taste to show too much sex

to the other side.' Is it (I was moved
to ask) nostalgic, tender, even raw
to look in later from a place apart?

Giving a low sigh, one spun and then spoke:
'The convocation of qualms and kisses,
the regrets, the assembly of regrets

for those not loved, for those not loved enough,
and for those who should never have been touched
– what else in this death could be more poignant? –

nothing being left of what might have been
but a half glance through a glaze of silver...'
And here one stopped. No, one could not go on.

xx Flying

One said to me tonight or was it day
or was it the passage between the two,
'It's hard to remember, crossing time zones,

the structure of the hours you left behind.
Are they sleeping or are they eating sweets,
and are they wanting me to phone them now?'

'In the face of technological fact,
even the most seasoned traveler feels
the baffled sense that nowhere else exists.'

'It's the moving resistance of the air
as you hurtle too fast against the hours
that stuns the cells and tissues of the brain.'

'The dry cabin air, the cramped rows of seats,
the steward passing pillows, pouring drinks,
and the sudden ridges of turbulence...'

'Oh yes, the crossing is always a trial,
despite precautions: drink water, don't smoke,
and take measured doses of midday sun,

whether an ordinary business flight
or a prayer at a pleasure altar...
for moments or hours the earth out of sight,

the white cumuli dreaming there below,
warm fronts and cold fronts streaming through the sky,
the mesmerising rose-and-purple glow.'

'So did you leave your home à contrecoeur?
Did you leave a life? Did you leave a love?
Are you out here looking for another?

Some want so much to cross, to go away,
somewhere anywhere & begin again,
others can't endure the separation...'

One night, the skyline as I left New York
was a garden of neon flowerbursts –
the celebration of a history.

XXIV Blind Date

'A date with life is a blind date with death.'
'Oh but a date with life is also blind.'
So who, I said then, makes the bitter choice?

'Do you picture *us* up here at the wheel?
We've never met the Driver either, dear.'
'But in all events, this is our advice:

Wear fine underthings in the street. You *can't*
cross wearing tatty lace or torn nylons.
Naked is better! For who ever knows

the moment the method the medium.'
'Oh dress well to meet your Match and Maker.
Clothes make the man! (*we* paraphrase Shakespeare).'

'Your last mirror may well be a rearview,
a compact, a cruiser, a glint of chrome
on a bathroom floor or on a bumper.'

'– Though some prefer the mirror of a lake,
the hues and phases of a lake or sea.'
Then one laughing began to lullaby:

'*How do you seem in silver blue or glow*
in glints of green or bloom in muddy brown
or blush in sunset rose or feel in fog?'

'Yes, always travel in your best attire,
inner and outer (both garter and gloves),
and never flash a ragged fingernail

at a gliding boat or a cruising car
(for the Dead have their own deadly standards).'
'*Wear a summer moon wear a silver star*

a gleam a glint of frost a fleck of dew
a glowwood glare sport moonrays in your hair.'
'No, never forget who and where you are.'

74

XXV   Poison Apples

'Love you to death,' one said tonight. Such grand
promises. And will you love me after?
'I will love you even ever after.'

A comfort abstract but no less complete.
It was far better it then seemed to me
to be loved in the dark by some unknown

– some virtual or relative unknown –
with ideal awe and miscomprehension
than to be loved as who I am and was,

for real, in all my real and rich detail,
who ate the rosy halves of several
poison apples from the hand of the Queen.

'…Yes, those who live best live in make-believe…'
'…to live well is to play it well, yes, yes…'
'…where believing is almost becoming…'

'…at our best in perpetual low light…'
But all Blanche's low lights and pure desires,
no, could never make her Snow White again

despite the fairest mirror on the wall
for the poor fair girl got lost in the Wood
and turned then to the kindness of strangers.

'Love us oh love us,' one said, 'if you will.'
It would be a devotion of the kind
'reserved for gods' or – who knew? – 'for angels'.

And just then I saw that the red of dawn
had lacquered the boughs of the apple trees
and painted a blush on the frozen snow.

XXVI Motherlessness

'We're referring to those with primal holes,
those whose souls were improperly sutured
in that so delicate time after birth

when the soul is as fragile as the skull
and calls for a mother's tender stitches...'
'No, of course we mean to say *anyone's.*'

'Leaving a hole in the skin of the soul,
a hole in the soul that should be a whole
(yes, please forgive this tired old homonym)

or several holes out of which it leaks...'
'So even the sparest nuance of wind
is a feeling, and in cases like those,

can you conceive of a sexual touch?'
'The mothered ones seldom consider how
they simply breathe the boon of love and blood;

those are the lucky ones, with whole smooth skins
like the spandex bodyskins of dancers.
The unmothered – no sooner do they sew

one gap shut than another hole opens,
for the fabric is fragile or brittle
and the person inside keeps pushing out

(the mere movement of life pushes or pumps).'
'*Can you dance in a bag? Dance in a rag?*
Are you living, darling, or are you dead?'

So what can be done for the sad unsewn
whose souls opened at birth but never shut?
Reluctantly, one murmured a reply:

'Oh weep, weep for them, for the leaking ones.
How close they really come in life to death...'
'All the looseness but not the liberty.'

XXVII Memory

'And do we remember our living lives?'
Did I remember the clock or the door,
or the words 'I love you' or the word 'why';
did he recall the blue vein in my wrist
or only the ice-blue burn in my eye?

What remained of the room and of the night,
the kiss or the argument that ensued?
'You see, our memories are much like yours,
here a shadow, a sound, a shred, a wisp...'
'And do we want to remember?' one said.

'Never never Oh give me the blurred wish
or the dream or the fact half-forgotten,
the leaf in the book but not the read page,
not what I saw but what I felt I saw,
not what I felt but how I wished to feel,

give me what I can bear to know I felt.'
I choose to recall only the blue dusk.
'Do you think you choose? If only you could
determine your secret determinants.'
Did I recall the cocktail as it smashed

against the wall there, so close to my eye,
did I forget why I left my home, why?
The full events of that terrible time
dissolving into the deep hues of dusk
and leaving essence to the inner eye.

XXIX Côte d'Azur

Out of the blue, one of them lipped to me:
'A handful of days can hold a whole life,
sunlight dazzling on a blue foaming sea,

the touch of a body and nothing more,
one whisper which was the very whisper
for which you had waited hour after hour,

maybe not the same words, not the same voice,
all those words other and voice still other,
the ring of unknown words, those were the ones.'

The hand that held my pen began to shine:
'How sad are those who borrow their solace
from several days never to return,

some incident of passion or promise,
some glimpse...' 'Oh yes, but sadder still are those
who never bask on even that brief beach.'

How blue the sea looked; it shone and *they* shone;
now they glittered with an utter glitter,
now they beamed, for this was their greatest *yes*.

'The special few are those who live full joys,
not a day, a week or a mooncycle
but an extension of years, or a life.'

'*Chimera on the surface of the sea,*
haze that lies heavy on a salty sea,
haze hovering over a summer sea,

despite the scintillations of the sun.'
'Where will all this lead? It will lead *nowhere*.
Nowhere at all is where we want to go.

A blue nowhere made up of blue nothing,
a moment of bliss lasting a moment,
long enough for life, that long and no more.'

from **SECOND ROUND**

XXXII   **A Well**

For a year I had tried to shake them off
but then found I had only left myself,
"high and dry" – dry, without a source. Had I

hoped their words rose from my own source, my well?
'But all the voices rise from "somewhere else"…
A "new" voice can be shrill and thin, but one

that has flo-flowed…' (the word came drifting up)
'through sev-er-al ve-ssels' (what did one mean?)
'is res-on-ant re-si-du-al and real.'

(I heard my father laughing: 'Well, well, well…')
'Yes, we like an "old" voice or a torrent
a chorus welling washing through one pipe

all at once through one throat in a temple
yes *a cappella* singing as though one.'
At last the words rose through me "swimmingly".

It was not a question of 'former lives'
or of 'future lives', since '*now is ever*'.
As always it was 'water and the sense

of water a teardrop a pane of glass
a glass half full or…' Here one swallowed hard.
'All clear, cross-lucent or clairvoyant things,

all things that waver or that well like waves,
all things through which some "other" shines or shows…'
And now the gurgle of a silly song:

'*Fear tears pour cold from the middles of eyes*
Joy tears are warm & slip from the corners
Anguish tears are salty & scald the cheeks

But love tears pool & glisten in the lids.'
The mirror flattened; the room was glazed and soft.
We were "one" again. I had sourced myself.

79

XXXIII Waiting

'What's the heaviest word in the language?'
'*Wait.*' 'Oh, but *want* is heavier than *wait.*'
'But *want* with *wait* is even heavier.'

'What's the lightest word?' '*Wit, white.*' 'A white fence,
a white page, a cloud...' 'The white of an egg,
the white of an eye...' 'The wink of an eye

is as heavy as *white*...' 'White of wisdom,
white of wit.' There's dark wisdom too. 'Yes, yes.'
I went to bed; I waited in the dark.

'How long did you wait?' I waited, I said.
'Oh, how long will you wait?' I'll wait, I said.
'A wanton wish, or an unwonted want?'

'A dark wish. *Want* is the work of the heart.'
In my dream, I weathered a "wall of wind".
Wall-eyed & wallflower, well of tears, wall.

'But *wait* can also be the lightest word.'
'*Wait* with *wish*?' 'With the wisp of a wish or
worlds of wishfulness.' Though what's in a word?

'Are you waiting for a weather report?'
'The weather of desire? The famous wings?'
Not 'the wings of...', but 'waiting in the wings'.

'*Some like a whistle, some want a wave,*
some like a window, some like a whip,
some want words, some like wind & water.'

Then I heard a laugh. 'We've lived many lives.'
'Those who remember them are lost in life.'
'Do you loathe lilies? The scent of perfume

on the day of your shame in 1201.
Do you despise the taste of caraway?
They plied you with aquavit till you "sang".

Do you hate pork? There was nothing but pig
and cabbage the winter of 405.'
'The most memorious are the most mad.'

'Mad ones revisit their ancient troubles.'
'Mad ones relive their former tragedies.'
But is there a cure, I wanted to know.

'There is no cure – the cure was *love at birth*.'
'Birth love seals the vestigial memories.'
Now is 'late in the day'. Now is 'too late'.

'Sad fact.' 'Sorry, sorry,' more than one said.
'But you,' one argued, 'have been soothed and spared.'
The pig and the lily are 'just a hint'.

'Lilies that fester,' another said this.
Caraway: '*Swing low*,' one began to sing.
'*Carry me away on the Waters of Life*...

Who blushed for you as the calyxes fell?
Who kissed your toes as she emptied the flask?
Who held the scented hankie to your nose?'

XXXV Yes

Every now and then one would blurt out *yes!*
A splurt of a *yes*, or a small *hurrah*.
What did I want? A 'reverie a day',
a 'flag', a 'flower', a 'flock of hellos'?

Did I expect 'bliss'? Did I, did I? *Yes.*
I longed for the river of what they were
to flow through the channel of what I was.
'And say what?' one said. 'We've said it *all*.

We've given you a century, a day...'
A flag flapping, the crowd cheering, bright light
rebounding off the flagpole; rising wind,
a heart lifting full of old-fashioned hope,

a halo, first gold, now made of rainbows.
So was there a choice? Could I choose my hat,
my hope? The crowd roared and tossed its halos.
The air shone and sparked with spinning prisms.

Was there a 'choice that lay behind the choice'
I 'seemed to have chosen' but 'never chose'?
Was it both 'prismatic' and 'pragmatic',
would it 'outlast the recent century',

and was the reverie 'reverential',
what was the 'river', and *which* was the 'bed',
and *which* day in *which* century would keep?
(The wind flagged as the dusk began to sift.)

The essential choice was 'the sense of choice',
the essential sense was 'the hat and hope'.
'*Are you in yourself when we are in you,*
& who are you within when we are you?'

XXXVI It

'We mean we never had a word to say.'
It was the sound of the word they liked or
if not the 'word' then the 'flow of the words'

'flowing together, petal by petal',
as though they carried the 'flux of a life' –
the 'stream that flows through us when we feel touched'.

'Remember that day, the day of his death,
the "lady of god", yes, when she touched you
a stream of cool water slipped through her hands?'

Yes? 'She did not say Jesus or Buddha...'
(Though 'what's in a name?') 'No, she did not say
you may call him what you will, call him *It*.'

What was that sense? 'It was the sense of *It*,
meaning the sense of nothing with a name
that you would never give for nothingness.'

'A sort of *It*, not sex, not secret love,
not cultish love: the rose of creation.'
'Just the concentrated flow of a force,

and the sense of fragrance without a smell,
the sense of a flavor without a taste.'
'*The elixir of concentrated life.*'

'A sound like a voice, one of those voices
you could breathe or eat, a voice you could kiss.'
And what was the essence of having *It*?

'*Our cool glow, our golden rose, our halo,
our sun as dark gold as gold leaf. Our* It.'
That was the day he died, he had gotten

It. 'Our word so late in the day, our *It*.
A word, whatever word, it says *It It*
our word it says what it will, it says *It*.'

XXXVII   **Hats**

'Oh, how we love the glow of holy gold!'
They curled, cavorting in the evening sun.
'Oh, but centuries have passed since the rage
for halos.' 'Yes, they're out of fashion now.'

'The angels have departed, and auras
may now be had and read in many hues.'
'Some see the shine on the heads of others,
others read luminations in themselves.'

'Yes, now we have the hues of bliss and wit,
and awkwardness and intuition, yes...'
I saw a violet sign that shone and hissed;
it gleamed like neon in the dropping dusk.

I had wished for a tender poets' blue,
but here was the hue of enlightenment.
The sign scrolled out *NARAN*, my spirit name.
'Why wish,' one turned and hissed, 'why wish, why wish?'

It was gentian blue; it was indigo;
it was myrtle or mauve, a rose-blue vein;
the silver blue of oysters on the half;
ink smeared thin across a violet sky.

It was a distillate of Dusk, a sign
that I was seeing and that I was seen.
'What's the fashion in hats?' 'No hat at all.'
'Oh, stylists try, but hats just don't come back!'

'And those who like to read luminations
do so on bare or bald or hatted heads.'
'Mad as hatters, we love the hidden hues!'
'Yes, the seventh sense is *also* color.'

XXXVIII   A Leaf

ADDRESS ME, I said, and I meant "please speak".
'Oh you mean *UNDRESS ME*,' one said and turned.
Had I meant "take off my dress"? 'What,' said one,

'is your address?' My dress was green as moss,
as pine, as weed, as seafoam, as a leaf.
What did I say? I said *GREEN AS A LEAF*

not *GREEN AS BELIEF*. Belief was 'a leaf
no one should wear'. 'Take off belief and wear
a dress.' Belief was 'no address at all'.

'Undress & address your audience.'
YES, UNDER DURESS I HAVE BEEN UNDRESSED.
I SAW THE LEAVES BECOME A NEST OF SNAKES;

I WATCHED THE SNAKES ENACT A SWARM OF HANDS.
Was there a sign on a blown-over leaf,
was there some inner palmistry or plan?

Here was a question 'not to be undressed'.
There was nothing to do but to revert
to a state of address before belief.

Here was the hand, the *feuille effacée.*
'Turn a new leaf,' one said, 'and turn a cheek.
Shed leaves, shed tears. *REDRESS YOURSELF.*'

XXXIX A Pea

Late one green night. Now me: Like the princess,
I bruise as I ride on the pea-green sea.
'It was a pea-green boat,' one said. 'The fog

is thick as...soup.' 'You're splitting...*never mind.*'
(The puns were flying now.) 'But is there *peace*
or *appeasement?*' Then this: 'No, only peas,

and on a rare night, green cheese.' Now one droned:
'*We like pale cheesy green, despite the face*
owling in the dark...we like earthen &

unearthly greens: leaves, moss, emeralds,
seaweed...green stars, green peas...the princess
bowing in her green gown & grinning CHEESE.'

And this: 'We never meant to go to sea.'
'Chlorophyll and oxygen, our favorite foods.'
There wasn't much peace as we spooned up soup.

'Do you want some advice?' one (sipping) said.
'Emulate the traits of pussies and owls.'
Four-footed and wingèd? 'No, lovable

and wise.' What about the princess? I said.
Did the pea make her arrogant and mean?
Did the pea make her hate the life she lived?

With time, she had learned 'not to blame the pea
for her nervous vulnerability...'
'or the mattress'...and to 'bruise gracefully'.

XL **Garden**

One crooned in my ear; I was waking up.
'Why insist that Eden was a Garden
with an apple, a lady and a snake?'

Then one: 'Snow White bit an apple and blushed
to death.' Then one: 'Not the apple-a-day-
that-keeps-the-doctor-away.' And: 'The snake

was a garden worm in her mother's eye.'
Her eye was a garden? I said and smirked.
'Any eye is Eden or a Desert.'

'Yes, the difference is a *UNIVERSE*.'
'Though a *verse* is a *turn*,' one (tartly) said,
'*return*, you'll note, has never meant *reverse*.'

'*Can she go back & eat the yellow half?*
Can she go back & never eat at all?
Can she turn the dark Queen into Glinda

with a click of red heels & a blown kiss?'
No, not in all the 'versicles of hope'
if 'seven little men' had 'tried and failed'.

And this was the 'meaning' of *UNIVERSE*:
'one-turn-forward and there's-no-going-back'.
And return is 'always a compromise',

like 'go home to Eden and wear a dress'.
Or only in the mirror on the wall
in which she lives 'the fairest life of all'.

XLI Murder

'Oh, murder!' she was heard to mutter, or
'Mary mother of god!' You see how close
these utterances come? Please *kiss me* Mom.

'Dial M for melancholy.' (Pity me.)
'Dial M for misery & M for muse.'
Of the several choices, I choose muse,

though I'd like an evening with Ray Milland,
the kind of murderer most girls desire,
the kind of *kill me* we might murder for.

'You know *mutter* is a word for *mother*
whereas *murmur* might be a mom we want.'
'Are you dying, dear, for a cup of milk?'

'Dial M for the milk of mother's love.'
'What other milk, we ask, is such a must?'
'An M won't buy you whiskey or water.'

'Dial M for Medea, who butchered her
babies to settle a score with their dad.'
I'd rather dial M for Ray Milland.

'Isn't that the point? So would she, my dear.
(May we remind you, hell hath no fury.)'
Was that the murder motive, jealousy?

Dial M for me & M for what I am,
a girl with no mother to dial for.
A girl whose mother was her murderer.

XLII Dreamorama

'Dream yr dreams,' one said. 'Silly, isn't it?
Most think this means *fulfill yr ambitions.*
Wrong! It means *dream yr dire, exotic dreams...*'

'Here's a new technotherapy,' one said.
'Scan yr mind's eye view for doctors and friends.'
'Not enough RAM to store the stuff in yr

mind? Store yr overflow in cyberspace.'
'Not enough time for precious R.E.M.?
Store contents, view later.' Now another:

'Oh, still at issue: how to avoid dream
data fragmentation during transfer...'
'*HEAD* line of the morning *ETHERPAPER*:

ANOTHER DREAM DOSSIER BURSTS, SCATTERS'
Images tumble through the outer space,
'diving' and 'tripping' over the airwaves,

'full-formed' or 'fragmented' or 'disfigured',
'gaudy or gleaming, pastel or grayed-out'.
The outer space scrambles with inner space...

'A TOE SOME TRASH A TOADSTOOL A TATTER
TREACHERY A TREAT A TREATISE A THREAT'
'*Night flowers flying on the wanton wind.*'

They thought they were funny. Were they funny?
'A DRAM A DRUG SOME DROOL A BIT OF DIRT
A DRAMA DELIRIUM DREAD A DRAG

A DALLIANCE A DEATH A DART A DIG'
'Don't like yr images? Re-envisage.
Faller, flyer? Revamp yr inner arc.

Don't dig the feeling? Redesign the frame.'
'Ha,' one said, 'a dream beyond ambition:
reconfigure yr DRAMAS & TRAUMAS.'

XLIII Moon Song

Once we met on a night without a moon.
'You don't need a moon to feel the longing,'
one said. 'All earthly matter is moonstruck.

Aren't we all moon-babies? Aren't all earthlings
moon-mavens?' And then this: 'Our most human
feature is mooning.' But what about dogs,

I said. Don't dogs moon? 'No, dogs *bay* at moons.'
'*Stare, stare at the cold green face of the moon.*
Why, there's nothing there, no grass, no trees,

and certainly no cheese...' 'That goes unsaid.'
'We gaze toward Otherness, as in *the grass
is always greener on the other side.*'

'Mooners that we are our fate is lunar.'
(They like a rhythm, they like a rhyme.) Why?
'Because complacency is a fat cow

chewing grass as it lows in a meadow.'
'Going to the moon won't get us our moon,
no thank you, Mr Glenn, any more than

surgery will cure heartache.' And then this:
'Oh leave us our golden calves and moon songs.'
And now seven slipped shining into song:

'*You've seen a blood-red moon, you've seen it green,
you've seen it white as ice and ringed in mist,
a gray face floating on a rosy sea.
Have you seen a blue moon? I saw one "once".
I saw a yellow moon* out of the blue.'

XLIV Three Green Stars

Was it an admission of arrogance
to say right out that I had visitors?
We were driving in the Jersey meadows,

a gray purple sky, roving orange spots,
white clouds lit miasmic yellow. 'It might
be best,' one said, 'to call us a conceit.'

The road flares rayed; the dotted lines spun smooth.
Another: 'Arrogance is like conceit.'
'Knowing of the movements of molecules,

who dreams that what you see is what you get?'
'No, what you see is never what you get.'
Another: '*Seeing isn't believing* –

and *out of sight* is never *out of mind.*'
'It's arrogant to reduce the wonders
of the universe to the size of your

sciences and fictions.' A sigh, a cough.
Three green stars frisked on the skyline. And then:
'What *crank* called this chaos a *UNIVERSE*?

One turn of a wheel? *One turn* of a thought?'
'At the helm of a roving Satellite,
a hand on a handle is *cranking* out

electrons, monads, endorphins & mist,
duendes & dreams, quarks, quirks,
ions & eons, beams & rays,

atoms & daimons, spots & dots.'
'Be humble,' one mewed. I hung to the wheel.
'Matter or not, it's all material.'

XLVI Yvoire

We'd been at Yvoire on the other shore,
where the lake mirrored a "tender" pink sky:
two plates of filet, a flask of pink wine,

a rag of pink cloud, a ribbon of wind...
'Pink,' one said, 'is still the color of love.'
Was this 'simile' or 'syllogism'?

These were 'unlike things alike in color'.
'Oh cultivate softness & subversion.
Oh succor sensuality & fact.'

What fact? I asked. What facet of a fact?
'Oh, love his girlish shame and his pink cock,
love his pink nipples, the scar on his cheek.'

The 'symmetry' is the 'synecdoche',
part for a whole as in *sail for a ship*,
where the pink evening and the pink filets

are the 'emblems of a sensual fact'.
What faction or refraction of a fact?
'The heart,' one said, 'is the throne of all joy.'

'It's a muscle,' one said, 'a piece of meat.'
Was one facetious? Here was the refrain:
'Is there juice, is there joy & jouissance,

is there manna & music & money?'
Could I face him and could I face myself?
'Oh, facsimile is as real as fact.'

XLVII Shangri-la

'Abortion, so what? Souls shed like old skin.
A moment later, one might have attached
to a Sherpa – a Sinbad – a Shiva –

a Scheherazade –' Why all the *shhhhs*?
'For the hush that ushers in the choice.'
We'd been climbing all day in nipping cold.

'Some are dry and yellow like old paper,
some are sweet and damp like cherry petals.'
'As molecules move, thus do souls.' ' – As sperm,

as atoms – remember your Lucretius...'
'And none is worth a shred, a scrap, a jot
until one sticks...' The air was cold and sharp.

'When the story begins, it must resolve...'
'A universal law.' ('A *flaw*,' one hissed.)
'If one sticks too long, the story begins,

and then *grief to all* on letting go.' 'No,
there's nothing holy in a particle.'
'What about the Uterus it clings to?'

'And a condom – wouldn't that have helped?'
I wonder if I wouldn't have preferred,
in my life, I said, some other Hostess.

'Hush,' one said, 'there is no Preferment.'
We had come to Shangri-la: falling snow,
medallions of frost and ash, glassy tears,

dewstars and dustflakes and cherry petals
clinging and melting on the mountainside.
O Confetti of our "created" world.

XLVIII   A Bug

Hot late summer: the dry leaves made no sound.
The only sound was the step of a foot
on the porch boards and then a shout: 'WE DON'T

EAT BUGS!' The baby wept, the baby screamed.
And then: 'SPIT THAT OUT!' The bug lay vicious
on her tiny tongue. Yes, the bug had juice,

the bug had love. But to make the bug love
her was the work of years. A small voice said,
'Turn it to gold and let it fly.' And yet

a century crept by before the bug
turned to gold. A hot sun *jaundiced* the porch,
the trees, board by board and leaf by leaf. Or

was the word *burnish*? Did it *burnish* them?
So that her rankest thoughts by turning gold
"became" her, or beautified her as she

became. She knew the phrase 'a heart of gold',
but other organs could be golden too.
'To a Flying enemy make a Bridge

of Gold.' One said that long ago, but make
your enemy into a golden bridge?
So late, a sense of what might matter and

what shouldn't; a place where a ring, a glint,
a tuft of blond hair, the rim of a cloud,
a gold leaf, a bottle cap all bask in

the damasked memory of the golden forms;
where all things and thoughts show how well she glows.
By now the bug had flown; so had the years.

XLIX Ellipses

Why was a *sole* an *only* and a *foot*?
And why was *soul* not *solar*, not *solid*?
Alone I was 'yes, a solipsism',
lips stammering alone (do you read that?);

I opened my lips, hoping one would speak.
As always they 'preferred the passages'
between 'no and yes', between 'dark and bright',
'those rays of the sun from behind the earth',

never the 'eye of the sun', its 'sham truths',
its illusion of 'seeing all'. They loved
all verges, the Dusk, the Dawn, the dusky
grays, the grayed and shadowed hues, all shadows

and ellipses (here were my lips again),
lulls, lapses, what was lost or left unsaid
or stated elsewhere; leaps of faith and love,
love, leaps of love, lips (read mine, I said),

the gentle attraction of gravity,
gradations and degrees, stairwells and steps,
hallways, hellos, and even some farewells:
all that led elsewhere and was else than self;

the object not the subject, the other
not the one. They endorsed Desire, this was
their Desideratum, *ipso facto*
(could these be lips again? read mine, I said);

all things 'through which some other showed or glowed'.
They loved 'a shingle hanging on a door',
a shiver, a sheer dress, a burst of song,
two shadows overlapping on a wall;

all things that 'transited toward Otherness',
'transitional, translucent, in a trance';
desire 'because it tended somewhere else'.
They 'shunned all certainties and forecasts'

(in this they were like me; we shared these thoughts);
nothing was known, this they were sure they knew;
and 'if anyone knew', it might be them.
The sun was eyeing us; I lapsed and slept.

95